ENKINDLED

Holy Spirit, Holy Gifts

Albert Haase, O.F.M.
Bridget Haase, O.S.U.

To John and Kathy
May you burn with the
gift of The
Spirit.
Bridget

ST. ANTHONY MESSENGER PRESS

Cincinnati, Ohio

Nihil Obstat: Rev. Ralph J. Lawrence
　　　　　　　Rev. Nicholas Lohkamp, O.F.M.

Imprimi Potest: Rev. Fred Link, O.F.M.
　　　　　　　Provincial

Imprimatur: +Most Rev. Carl K. Moeddel
　　　　　　　Vicar General and Auxiliary Bishop
　　　　　　　Archdiocese of Cincinnati
　　　　　　　September 18, 2000

The *nihil obstat* and *imprimatur* are a declaration that a book is considered to be free from doctrinal or moral error. It is not implied that those who have granted the *nihil obstat* and *imprimatur* agree with the contents, opinions or statements expressed.

Scripture citations are taken from the *New Revised Standard Version of the Bible*, copyright ©1989 by the Division of Christian Education of the National Council of Churches of Christ in the U.S.A. Used by permission. All rights reserved.

Cover photography Copyright ©Don Farrall/PhotoDisc/PictureQuest
Cover design by Constance Wolfer
Book design and production by Sandy L. Digman

ISBN-13: 978-0-86716-409-1
ISBN-10: 0-86716-409-3

Published by St. Anthony Messenger Press
28 W. Liberty St
Cincinnati, OH 45202
www.SAMPBooks.org

Printed in the U.S.A.

11 5 4 3

# Come, Holy Ghost

COME, HOLY GHOST, Creator blest,
And in our hearts take up thy rest;
Come with thy grace and heav'nly aid
To fill the hearts which thou hast made.

O, COMFORTER, to thee we cry,
Thou heav'nly gift of God Most High;
Thou fount of life, and fire of love,
And sweet anointing from above.

O HOLY GHOST, through thee alone,
Know we the Father and the Son;
Be this our firm unchanging creed,
That thou dost from them both proceed.

PRAISE WE THE LORD, Father and Son,
And Holy Spirit with them one;
And may the Son on us bestow
All gifts that from the Spirit flow.

— *Attributed to Rabanus Maurus, 776-856;*
  translated by Edward Caswall, 1814-1878

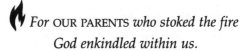 *For* OUR PARENTS *who stoked the fire*
God enkindled within us.

Contents

Introduction

One theologian has called the Holy Spirit the "neglected middle child" of the Blessed Trinity. Unfortunately, that description has merit. While every Sunday we profess our faith in the "Lord and Giver of Life," most of us would be hard pressed to say anything significant about the Spirit that goes beyond the traditional image of the dove.

Enkindled: Holy Spirit, Holy Gifts is our attempt to bring this "neglected middle child" front and center and to address the void in popular reading about the Holy Spirit and the seven gifts of the Spirit. These chapters originally appeared in a different form in a monthly column in *St. Anthony Messenger* magazine in 1998.

The book consists of twelve short chapters. The first two introduce one way of understanding the Spirit and the seven gifts. The next seven chapters focus on each of the individual gifts of the Holy Spirit. Chapters Ten and Eleven illustrate how the fruits of the Spirit help us overcome fear and desire, the two major challenges in spiritual growth. The final chapter suggests that prayer is the most common way to stoke the fire of the Spirit in our lives.

Each chapter consists of a short reflection, three questions for discussion and personal meditation, and a prayer.

We wrote *Enkindled* for people who reflect while commuting to work; for those who pray while the baby is sleeping; for those who belong to parish discussion groups and the Rite of Christian Initiation of Adults; for those preparing to receive the Sacrament of Confirmation and for those who celebrate the divine generosity of the Gift-Giving Spirit.

Our hope is that through reading, personal reflection and prayer, all of us might daily feel the warmth of the fire that God, out of utter generosity and boundless love, lit inside each of us the day we rose from the waters of Baptism. That fire penetrates all creation and unites us to each other—and to God.

Albert Haase, O.F.M.
Beijing, People's Republic of China

Bridget Haase, O.S.U.
Dedham, Massachusetts

Pentecost 2000

CHAPTER ONE

Fire of Love, Breath of Life

From the moment they met in freshman algebra class, something "clicked" between Troy and Andrea. Within one week, they were eating lunch together and enjoying life in a way they had never before experienced. Within six weeks, the topic of their nightly phone calls switched from math homework to talk of "us," "our relationship" and "what's going on between us."

Troy and Andrea were experiencing one of life's great events—and one of the most concrete experiences of God's presence in our lives: one's first love.

Electricity of Love

When two people fall in love, something like "electricity" arises between them. It bonds their relationship like Super Glue in such a way that the couple begin to talk about themselves using new inclusive pronouns, *we* and *us*. It's as if their love, their relationship—that "electricity"—has taken on an identity all its own, making the two of them one flesh. In marriage, that new identity is frequently celebrated in the birth of a child.

Though the love-relationship analogy has its limitations when speaking of the Trinity, it gives us an intuitive sense of the Holy Spirit's place in the trinitarian life of God. The Holy Spirit proceeds from the loving, eternal reciprocal gaze between the Father and the Son. The Spirit is that "fire of love," to quote the words of the hymn, "Come, Holy Ghost," that is enkindled between them and seals their relationship from and for all eternity.

As the "fount of life," another title from the traditional hymn, the Spirit is breathed into Adam and Eve, making each of them and their descendants "a temple of the Holy Spirit" (see 1 Corinthians 6:19). This same Spirit, in the form of a strong wind and tongues "as of fire," transforms a small community of confused believers into courageous preachers of the risen Christ and thus gives birth to the missionary charism of the Church (see Acts 2:3–4).

Feminine Life-Giver

A growing number of theologians, both male and female, speak of the Spirit using the third-person feminine pronoun. Four scriptural references suggest why.

The word *spirit* is a translation of the Hebrew *ruah*, a grammatically feminine noun, meaning "breath, air, wind"—the hovering wind of the Genesis creation account (see Genesis 1:2), the life-giving breath that God breathed into humanity (see Genesis 2:7).

In the Old Testament, the figure of Wisdom is often

personified as a woman. She lies at the very heart of life, penetrating and pervading all things (see Wisdom 7:24). She proceeds from God before all ages and is active in the work of creation (see Proverbs 8:22-31). Wisdom is God's "delight" as she plays before the Creator (Proverbs 8:30). She is traditionally associated with the Holy Spirit.

The New Testament tradition further alludes to the femininity of the Spirit. Luke, changing Matthew's Gospel which emphasizes the *descent* of the Holy Spirit at Jesus' Baptism, states explicitly that the Spirit descended upon Jesus *"in bodily form* like a dove" (Luke 3:22, italics added for emphasis). Perhaps Luke's emphasis on the physical form of the dove was to highlight to his Gentile audience the feminine character of the symbol, since in the world of his readers, the dove was the symbol of goddesses such as Astarte, Venus and Athena.

In Revelation, John has a vision of "the river of the water of life...flowing from the throne of God and of the Lamb.... On either side of the river, is the tree of life...producing its fruit each month" (Revelation 22:1–2). This river of life-giving waters, flowing from God and the Lamb's throne, clearly represents the Third Person of the Trinity. It calls to mind the life-giving waters of John's Gospel that also represent the Holy Spirit (see John 7:38–39). This river is a symbol of fertility, and in John's culture, goddesses were the agents of fertility.

Though words and images, drawn from human experience, are incapable of describing God accurately, the writers of Scripture evidently perceived what they considered to be a feminine quality in the Person and mission of the Holy Spirit.

Operating System of the Christian Life

The very word *spirituality* (spirit-uality) reflects the reality that, using the contemporary language of computers, the Holy Spirit is the "operating system" of a Christian's life. In the words of the *Catechism of the Catholic Church* (CCC), the Spirit is the "artisan of God's works" (#741). Saint Paul says, "We live by the Spirit, let us also be guided by the Spirit" (Galatians 5:25). As Wisdom herself proclaims, "For [the one who] finds me finds life..." (Proverbs 8:35).

In Baptism, the Spirit is poured into our hearts as an expression of God's boundless love for us (see Romans 5:5); in Confirmation, the Spirit is poured out completely and clothes us "with power from on high so that [we] may be [Christ's] witness[es]" (CCC, #1304). This divine presence within us gives us a share in Jesus' relationship with the Father, making us children of God and empowering us to call God "Abba" (see Romans 8:15–16).

Thus it is through the baptismal gift of the Holy Spirit that life and love are enkindled within us. We are formed into one family—"us"—and drawn into that endless, ecstatic love relationship of God called the Trinity. "All of us who have received one and the same Spirit, that is, the Holy Spirit, are in a sense blended together with one another and with God" (CCC, #738).

For Reflection

- *Have my experiences of love taught me anything about God? How have I experienced the Holy Spirit in them?*

- *In what ways is the Holy Spirit the "operating system" of my life?*

- *How do I see myself propelled by the winds of the Spirit to be a missionary among my family and friends?*

- *What makes me feel frightened or uncomfortable about this challenge?*

O BREATH OF LIFE, I look up to the heavens and feel your presence. Before the earth came to be, you were poured forth and were there when the skies were established. You existed before all ages, playing in delight before the Creator.

Yet this was not enough for you. You entered the clay of my being and set ablaze a fire of love. It is no longer you and I, but we.

Let me continue living and walking in your love, sharing its warmth with others. Stoke my fire with courage so that I may be an ember of justice and peace in an often indifferent world.

But, above all, deepen my trust in our unity so that with Jesus, I can confidently cry out, "Abba," today and every day. AMEN.

CHAPTER TWO

The Gift-Giving Holy Spirit

Lisa, a junior in college, was talking about her relationship with Joel, her boyfriend.

"There are times in our relationship when I feel like I'm in a sailboat. With a little bit of maneuvering, we easily catch the wind and are pushed along. During these times when we are 'clicking,' I realize again that our relationship is a pure gift from God.

"And yet, there are other times with Joel when I feel like I'm in a rowboat. It's hard work for me. I have to dig deep down inside myself and muster up strength and coordination to move the relationship forward. At these times, I realize that the gift of a relationship with Joel demands hard work. I have to use my talents, gifts and abilities to maintain and foster what we have started."

As Lisa talked, it dawned on me that her images of a sailboat and a rowboat are also apt when speaking of the Holy Spirit's relationship to us. The sailor's wind is like the free baptismal gift of the Spirit in the life of the Christian. The rower's strength and coordination are like the gifts of the Spirit that are freely, profusely and indiscriminately bestowed upon the baptized.

Sacramental Gifts of the Spirit

The seven sacraments are the preeminent gifts of the Holy Spirit at work within the communal relationship called the Church. The *Catechism* describes them as "the masterworks of God" (#1116). As such, they provide the strength and coordination for those in the rowboat, as well as the training and wind for those in the sailboat.

The sacraments of initiation—Baptism, Confirmation and Eucharist—"confer the graces needed for the life according to the Spirit during this life as pilgrims on the march towards the homeland" (*CCC*, #1533). Reconciliation, "through the blood of Christ and the gift of the Holy Spirit" (*CCC*, #827), frees the baptized from sin. The Anointing of the Sick bestows "a particular gift of the Holy Spirit" (*CCC*, #1520) that helps one to overcome the difficulties associated with serious illness or the frailty of old age. In the Sacrament of Holy Orders, the Spirit "configures" the ordained minister "to Christ as Priest, Teacher, and Pastor" (*CCC*, #1585). In Matrimony, the Holy Spirit is the seal of the spouses' covenant, "the ever-available source of their love and the strength to renew their fidelity" (*CCC*, #1624).

Charisms of the Spirit

But even the seven sacraments cannot contain the lavish generosity of the Spirit in the life of the Christian. The history of the early Church, especially at Corinth, gives witness to spiritual "gifts," or charisms, that are also a "manifestation of the Spirit" (see 1 Corinthians 12:4–11). Wisdom, knowledge, faith, healing, the working of miracles, prophecy, discernment of spirits, speaking in tongues and the interpretation of them are all Spirit-given abilities whose intended purposes go beyond the rational and individual to the relational and communal.

In a sense, they are not for the person in the sailboat or rowboat, but for the people on the ferryboat. They are given for the common good and are meant to build up the community as it journeys to the final shore.

Though the exercise of these spiritual gifts establishes a hierarchy of ministries within the Body of Christ (see 1 Corinthians 12:28), Saint Paul is adamant that they should not divide first-class from third-class passengers, captains from cabin attendants. Rather, they get helping hands on deck and drive the gifted into a deeper relationship with the community. Thus, Paul eloquently reminds the Corinthians that the exercise of these charisms without love is misguided, futile and worthless (see 1 Corinthians 13).

Seven Gifts of the Spirit

The traditional "seven gifts of the Holy Spirit," a term dating back to the second century, have their roots in Isaiah's description of the spiritual endowment of the promised messianic king. The Anointed One would receive "the spirit of wisdom and of understanding, the spirit of counsel and of strength, the spirit of knowledge and the fear of the Lord" (Isaiah 11:2). In the Greek Septuagint and Latin Vulgate translations of the Bible, the last gift, indicated by one Hebrew word used twice, was translated by two different terms—piety and the fear of the Lord—and thus the gifts became seven. This is a biblical number connoting abundance, fullness and plenitude rather than seven distinct gifts.

The history of Christian spirituality, however, has given considerable attention to these seven as distinct. One very early writer, for example, linked each to a specific Old Testament hero while another added to their number and noted their full realization in the person of Jesus. A fourth-century writer contrasted them with the Ten Commandments while, two centuries later, another writer connected them with the theological virtues. Thomas Aquinas, the great thirteenth-century theologian of the Church, viewed them as aids that expand human freedom and love, thus transforming the believer into a direct instrument of God's actions. Traditional manuals of Catholic spirituality in the twentieth century emphasized the fact that four of the gifts pertain to the mind while three pertain to the heart.

Today, unfortunately, these seven gifts do not get much attention. Indeed, discussion of them seems restricted to Confirmation preparation classes and the Rite of Christian Initiation of Adults. But they are still very active in our individual lives since they make us "docile in readily obeying divine inspirations" (*CCC*, #1831). In a nutshell, they are the extra spiritual "boost" that puts "a tiger in the tank" and enlightens us to the divine fire of life and love that burns within us and pervades everything that surrounds us.

In the following chapters, we'll take a look at each one of them individually.

For Reflection

- *When in my life have I experienced the Spirit as the sailor's wind and the rower's strength?*

- *How have I experienced the sacraments at work in my life? How have they challenged me to serve the community?*

- *How are particular gifts of the Holy Spirit active in my everyday life?*

O GIVER OF GIFTS, with each new dawn you invite me to catch the wind of your Spirit and journey farther in life-giving waters. I thank you for your graced gifts that enable me to row in life's undercurrents and sail its seas.

Challenged to build community as we ferry together, may I boldly proclaim your name and generously share what I have so lavishly received.

Make me strong enough to resist the temptation to seek a secure resting place and quiet enough to learn when to row and when to sail.

Renewing my fidelity to this journey, O God, encourage me to continue my way to the final port. And when my boat comes to shore, may it anchor in the harbor of your boundless love.

I ask this blessing in Jesus' name. AMEN.

CHAPTER THREE

The Gift of Wisdom

My Canadian neighbor, Eileen, was visiting me in my apartment. I wasn't surprised when Gong Jing, one of my students, showed up once again unannounced at my door. He reminds me so much of Nicodemus. He always comes to visit at night, filled with tough questions: How do you really know there is a God? Why is Jesus so important? Does faith really make a difference in a person's life? I dare not tell him—lest I scare him away—that his search for answers is already the beginning of his own pilgrimage of faith.

I always answer Gong Jing with the carefully crafted, finely nuanced answers of any other academician holding a Ph.D. in theology. And his response has always been the same: a blank face. This night, I was a little disappointed—yet relieved—that he directed his usual questions not to me but to my visitor, Eileen.

Using her thirty-five years of marriage to Alex as an example, Eileen spoke from her heart of her personal experience of God. She mentioned how, through daily prayer, she has discovered God's love for her made flesh in Alex and all his tinkering with leaking faucets. She talked about how her life of prayer and faith helped her to see Alex and their life together in ways her bifocals never could. She touched upon the different roles that Jesus played in her marriage: child psychologist, best friend and marriage counselor.

Gong Jing listened intently. And with each answer that Eileen gave, he nodded, letting his native Chinese slip from under his tongue, "*Wo ming bai le*," meaning "Yes, I see, I get it."

It didn't take me long to realize that Eileen had been graced with an extra dose of wisdom.

The Greatest of the Gifts

Most of us think of wisdom in the way a dictionary would define it: "understanding of what is true, right or lasting" or "common sense or good judgment." We think wisdom is centered upon the mind and see it exemplified in the scholar's ability to sift through the essentials of an erudite article, summarize it and apply it to daily life. But that is the "wisdom of this age" (see 1 Corinthians 2:6), and the Holy Spirit's gift of wisdom is something quite different.

Saint Paul describes the traditional understanding of this gift: "But, as it is written, 'What no eye has seen, nor ear heard nor the human heart conceived, what God has prepared for those who love him'—these things God has revealed to us through the Spirit; for the Spirit searches everything, even the depths of God" (1 Corinthians 2:9–10). The gift of wisdom is the fruit of a deep spiritual *experience*—not book learning—and consequently, it is centered upon the heart, not the mind.

The "heart" refers to that special treasure chest within each of us where our experiences of love and lessons from life are stored. It's where we "chalk up" experiences to life. It's the "place in the gut" that remembers the first kiss and the first betrayal, witnessing the birth of a child and the burial of a spouse. It's where we go to speak when we are ecstatic, the refuge we seek when we are depressed. It's the ground we stand upon when we want to make a good impression, the castle we protect when people speak harsh words. In a word, it's the "interior point" where we engage and experience life.

The Latin word for wisdom, *sapientia*, derived from the verb *sapere*, "to savor, to taste," suggests the heart is also the banquet table where our hunger and thirst for the ultimate in love and life—God—are satisfied. "O taste and see that the Lord is good" (Psalm 34:8).

Wisdom quenches our thirst for God in the way soft drinks and iced tea quench our thirst during summer. It not only satisfies our appetite for the things of God but also nourishes and expands it. One "knows" God as one knows a beloved spouse—not as a chapter in a history book, but as flesh and blood. Indeed, the Christian experiences God "in" the spouse.

The Spirit's gift of wisdom is the experiential knowledge of God that comes from an awareness and perception of God's encompassing presence in creation. It is Eileen's uncanny ability to have firsthand knowledge and intimate familiarity with the depths of God's love in her relationship with Alex. It is the experience of the extraordinary in the midst of the ordinary. In a word, it is Saint Paul's "seeing, hearing and feeling" the sacred as it peeks through the clouds of wedding vows, a helping hand and the majesty of creation. No wonder Thomas Aquinas considered wisdom the greatest and most perfect of all the seven gifts, the one embodying all the others.

Gift to All

There's no reason for us to be envious of people like Eileen, thinking they have a corner on the market. The Spirit has lavished this gift upon each one of us, though many of us never take the time to unwrap it. Our problem is that we are stuck upstairs—in our heads—where we can easily divide, categorize and compartmentalize everything with our dualistic distinction between the sacred and the secular. We need to "come down" to our hearts, to that inner space where we experience life. That's where the party is.

Walking down the stairs takes nothing more than "settling down" for a few moments each day as Eileen does. "Stop! Look! Listen!"—ageless advice for children and adults wanting to experience the thrills of the journey. A little bit of prayerful, quiet time every day goes a long way in clearing a path to that holy garden in our humdrum lives where the gift of wisdom is perennially blossoming. And it is there—which really is right here—where our hearts are enlightened to and set ablaze by "the fullness of him who fills all in all" (Ephesians 1:23).

For Reflection

- *How has my understanding of God changed over the years? How was God's gift of wisdom active in this discovery?*

- *When have I experienced God's presence in creation? What insights about my own place in creation did this experience provide?*

- *How can I plan more time for "seeing, hearing and feeling" the sacred in my everyday life? What paths need clearing? How does my "garden" need tending?*

O GOD OF WISDOM, yearning to quench my thirst, I longingly gaze up to the heavens. I sense your presence there but neither feel your breath nor hear your heartbeat. Empty words spring from parched lips and a dry spirit.

Grace me, O God, with your gift of wisdom. It will challenge me to get my head out of the clouds and follow the rain down here below. Only then will my heart rediscover the life-giving waters of love's experiences and life's lessons.

In quiet prayer let me become aware of your presence flowing in all creation as I behold the ordinary unfolding the extraordinary. My spirit will be satisfied as the drought of my mind yields to a savor in my heart, for once again I will see, feel and hear you everywhere, O Fount of Life, O Fire of Love. AMEN.

CHAPTER FOUR

The Gift of Understanding

I had always been curious about what it means to be made "in the image and likeness of God" (Genesis 1:27). My intuition had told me over the years that an important principle of the spiritual life was expressed in that statement, but I had not discovered it.

One day, while I was in a course on the doctrine of the Trinity, the professor offered a profound insight. He made the statement that the very essence of God is relational. The doctrine of the Trinity alerts us to the fact that the Father is only a father because he has a Son whom he loves; the Son is only a son because he has the Father whom he loves; the Father and Son share an intimate relationship of love because the Holy Spirit binds them together. God is a trinity of loving relationships that cannot be dissected. As John puts it so succinctly, "God is love" (1 John 4:8b).

The moment I heard that, bells went off in my head and my soul was flooded with light. "That's it!" I heard myself blurt out, much to the consternation of my classmates. One aspect of the divine imprint that we carry is our capacity and obligation to be in relationship to others, to open our hearts to them in compassion, to love them. Just as dimensions of God's divinity are revealed in the relationships of the Trinity, so, too, dimensions of our humanity are discovered when we reach out our hands and hearts to others. Indeed, only then do we discover who we really are: members of a family inextricably bound together because of the divine image and likeness stamped upon our souls.

Spiritual Insight

The Spirit's gift of understanding provides us with a special pair of glasses that helps us to move beyond statements on paper and see into the mysteries those statements profess. It gives us the ability to read "between the lines" and make connections that we may have never thought about in the past. It illuminates areas of our minds that are sometimes darkened by niggling questions or confusion. In summary, the gift of understanding offers spiritual insight that breaks through the blindness of our minds.

Though traditionally considered a gift bestowed upon the mind, understanding also touches the heart since it affects the way we engage and experience life. It provides *Eureka!* experiences, as it did for me that afternoon in the classroom, in which sparks of the Spirit set our lives ablaze, often renewing our vigor and enthusiasm for living an authentic life of faith.

Discovered in Reflection

This second gift of the Spirit, however, is not restricted to mysteries of our faith. The Spirit enkindles understanding whenever we take the time to examine our actions. It glows and even flares up at times when we stand before an experience in life and ask ourselves, "What's going on here?" "Why did I do that?" "How could I have allowed that to happen?"

A husband comes home from work. He snaps at his wife and brushes off energetic children who are happy to see him. Only later, mulling over his day, does he realize that his passive-aggressive behavior is the product of stress he has brought home from work.

A single woman finds herself often flirting with a coworker's husband. She sometimes feels ashamed, and yet is not aware of what is motivating her actions. After some honest self-reflection, she begins to see the effect her lonely life-style and lack of friends have on her—and how they could potentially affect a happy marriage.

A high school sophomore finds himself going along with the gang and experimenting with drugs. He doesn't really like it but doesn't know why he always gives in to peer pressure. After talking to the school counselor, he realizes that his need for acceptance among his friends is not as important as being in control of his own life.

When we take the time to think over our behaviors, perhaps in preparation for the Sacrament of Reconciliation, or try to learn from an experience, we often discover just how rich in understanding our lives really are.

The Understanding of Wounds

The helping professions are filled with people who use this gift to great advantage. Counselors, spiritual directors and people in self-help programs, such as Alcoholics Anonymous and Adult Children of Alcoholics, know well that the hurts and wounds they have caused or received are not dead-end streets. Hurts become holy ground and wounds become wisdom when we pause to ponder and understand them. We experience a gradual enlightenment as we realize, recognize and understand the reasons and hidden motivations for our own or others' actions. This kind of comprehension can put us waist-deep in compassion.

Understanding gives us the ability to accept others just as they are, to listen to them, to lovingly encourage and challenge them. Just like Jesus, we can "sympathize" with the weaknesses of others since we, too, have struggled with many of the same issues (see Hebrews 4:15). There is no greater consolation we can give to people drowning in sadness, guilt or confusion, than to say, "I've been there. I've done that. I know why." Compassion inflated with understanding is a life preserver we can hand others, offering them hope and new beginnings for the odyssey of life.

For Reflection

- *When did understanding help me to view a situation in life from a different perspective? How did that insight affect my subsequent decisions?*

- *When did my compassion offer another the hope of a new beginning?*
- *What personal hurts have become holy ground? What wounds of mine have been transformed into wisdom?*

O SPIRIT OF UNDERSTANDING, my heart's inner eye seems out of focus, for I can't read between the lines of life anymore. In my farsighted vision, I see only worries of the future or regrets of the past. And with bifocals, I magnify my own faults and those of others.

Break through my blurred vision, O Gracious God, with understanding's special pair of glasses. Sharpen my perception so that I may grasp the mystery of life's whole picture.

In compassion and encouragement let me open my heart and reach out my hands to others. Then will our common struggles become victories and our failures, sources of hope.

Like Mary, may I express understanding by standing under another's cross in a faithful embrace. AMEN.

CHAPTER FIVE

The Gift of Knowledge

I was sitting in the teacher's lounge, feeling sorry for myself and disillusioned. Despite all the careful preparation and planning, my four English discussion courses weren't going as well as I had planned.

While I was wrapped up in myself, my colleague, Zhang Wen, entered the room. Responding to her question, I told her I was doing "just fine," not wanting to share my self-pity with her. She proceeded to sit down and spontaneously started giving me some feedback about what she had heard about my courses. She told me how the students were enjoying the courses, how they felt challenged by them and how they kept bragging to others about all the idioms and useful English expressions they were learning.

As Zhang Wen talked, I felt the storm clouds of discouragement dissipate and my old upbeat self returning. When I asked her what brought all these compliments on, she replied, "I've been meaning to tell you, but just haven't found the right time. This morning when I came in here, something told me you needed some good news."

That "something" was the Holy Spirit's gift of knowledge.

Science of the Saints

The third gift of the Holy Spirit is often confused with philosophical or theological knowledge. But it's neither. It is not found in a textbook, written on the blackboard or received through our five physical senses. Rather, the gift of knowledge is what we learn in the classroom of the soul through an elusive sixth sense of the heart. It has traditionally been called the "science of the saints."

Those schooled in this holy science know that there is a knowledge that comes from keeping their ears to the ground and listening to the events in their lives. They approach life fully aware that there are facts that are imperceptible to the five senses and truths that cannot be explained by reason or logic. As the fox said to the Little Prince, "Only with the heart does one see rightly; what is essential is invisible to the eye." This gift is active in the life of anyone who is in touch with and sensitive to what is going on "below the surface" of a situation.

When our gut tells us that we have inadvertently hurt someone, when something tells us that a friend needs a hug, when we intuit a child's need for attention or affection, when we rightly suspect the source of a family member's pain or problem, we discover just how wonderful a gift knowledge really is.

The Family of Creation

Traditionally, knowledge also helps us rightly judge creatures in their relationship to God and ourselves. It acknowledges the limitation of created things to make us happy. Furthermore, it teaches us that all creatures are interrelated, forming one universal web of interdependent relationships. This marvelous web of creation binds us all together into one family and becomes a visible sign of a deeper, invisible reality—the perfection of our common Creator, the generous love of our gracious God.

Francis of Assisi is the classic example of a person who blossomed with this communal dimension of knowledge. He had an uncanny ability to see the familial bonds that united him with both the animate and inanimate. His famous song, "The Canticle of the Creatures," is a true celebration of the cosmic dimensions of the family of creation: He praises and sees God in Brother Sun, Sister Moon, Brothers Wind and Air, Sister Water, Brother Fire, Mother Earth, those who pardon and Sister Death. Furthermore, Brother Thomas of Celano, his first biographer, reminds us that Francis saw creation as a ladder pointing the way to the unseen Creator. "In every work of the artist he praised the Artist; whatever he found in the things made he referred to the Maker. He rejoiced in all the works of the hands of the Lord and saw behind things pleasant to behold their life-giving reason and cause. In beautiful things he saw Beauty itself; all things were to him good. 'He who made us is the best,' they cried out to him. Through his footprints impressed upon things he followed the Beloved everywhere; he made for himself from all things a ladder by which to come even to his throne" (Second Life, 165).

Today, those who approach their neighbor or the environment with love, reverence and respect manifest this aspect of knowledge. Ecologists, lovers, environmentalists and those who minister among minorities remind us that trees serve other purposes than just producing paper, there's more to love than good looks and sexual feelings, endangered species speak volumes about our failure as creation's stewards and our bonds as sisters and brothers run deeper than our white, black, yellow, brown or red faces.

With the gift of knowledge, we learn that there's more to life than meets the eye.

For Reflection

- *What has the "sixth sense" of the heart taught me about my family and friends?*

- *What personal obstacles of my heart hinder me from experiencing life "below the surface"?*

- *What message does my use of material possessions convey to others? How does knowledge lead me from the paper to the tree and from the sweater to the sheep?*

O GOD OF KNOWLEDGE, in praise and gratitude I accept your gift of knowledge within my spirit. With it you enable me to read the big print and skim the fine of my life's book. May your grace teach me that all my chapters form the one universal story of your lavish love and gentle care.

School me beyond the science of written pages to the sensitivity of inner vision. May my life itself become an enfleshed message of love, reverence and respect for you and all of creation.

With Saint Francis, I join my prayer to his celebration of all creatures. AMEN.

CHAPTER SIX

The Gift of Counsel

A nthony and Jill were the best of friends for their first two years of high school. But once Mark entered Jill's life, Anthony started to feel the distance between Jill and himself. That saddened him.

Anthony was also confused by the drastic change in Jill's behavior. She began to smoke cigarettes as Mark did. Formerly a conscientious and hardworking student, Jill started missing classes. Anthony noticed that Mark was also absent at those times.

Anthony was convinced that Mark was a bad influence on Jill. But should he mention this to Jill? Should he mind his own business? Was he simply jealous of their friendship? Or was his motivation based upon wanting the very best for someone whom he still considered a friend?

As he agonized over whether or not to talk to Jill, Anthony prayed for guidance to make the right decision.

Tough Questions

Should I tell a friend that I fear someone is a bad influence upon her? Can I keep quiet about some questionable practices in which my business is involved?

Is this the person that I'm supposed to marry and be with for the rest of my life? Should I uproot my family and accept the transfer to another city? Should we try again to have a baby on our own or adopt?

Some questions can be so agonizing because we are all too aware that decisions can be made for the wrong reasons, or even worse, mistakes can be made. It's quite simple to pretend to know what and who is best for those we love. It's so much easier to be an innocent bystander rather than to rock the boat and be the lone prophetic voice of dissension. We know how wealth and beauty can sometimes attract us to the wrong prospective spouse. Career decisions are easily negotiated for selfish reasons without due consideration to the immediate family or extended family obligations. The decision to become a parent is heavy with responsibilities and demands a lot of personal maturity.

In a word, the flimsy, selfish concerns of the ego can seduce us into making misguided and sometimes even devastating decisions.

Right Judgment

The fourth gift of the Holy Spirit, the gift of counsel, helps us make decisions properly and wisely. It is the heavenly floodlight that shines on us as we survey our history, our motivations, our talents and our desires in the face of an important decision. It is the compass and map that God gives to us when we stand at a crossroads in life. It is the help we get to "size up" a situation, to put things into perspective, to discern alternatives, to see the ramifications and consequences of each choice. With counsel, we are given the ability to rightly judge how to *respond* to a situation, not simply *react* to it.

Counsel is the gift that helps us haul the ego, heavy and clumsy as it sometimes is, out of the decision-making progress. It unmasks other obstacles like rashness, hesitation, procrastination, negligence, rationalization, inconstancy and presumption that often fog up our glasses and delay or hinder a clear-sighted decision. It creates an inner space where decisions can be prudently and freely made.

Components of Decision-Making

This gift of the Spirit aids us in making the right decision for the right reason. Sometimes it comes to us like lightning out of nowhere as we "think through" the haze of choices and consequences. Sometimes it comes in dialogue with family, friends, trusted advisers, spiritual directors or *counselors*. In either case, it keeps before our eyes the elements of a wise, prudent decision.

Counsel aids hindsight so I can look honestly at my "track record." Any prudent decision acknowledges that past choices have already paved a path and sent me in a certain direction. They consequently have created an environment that will have some influence and effect upon the future. The future is a blossom of the past, not a graft onto it.

This gift sheds light on my present situation and circumstances with all of their commitments and responsibilities. It reminds me of promises and obligations that may be binding for both today and tomorrow. The journey forward starts from where I am now.

Flying With Feet on the Ground

Counsel helps us see our God-given gifts and talents that make us "diamonds in the rough" and that, up to now, may have gone unnoticed. These potential skills and abilities are wings that help us fly over brick walls and maneuver around obstacles that our past and present sometimes put in our way. They also help us be creative in responding to God's unique call to holiness for each one of us.

As I soar with my talents, counsel also keeps my feet on the ground. It reveals to me which hopes and dreams that fuel my "get up and go" are realistic and achievable. It also informs me which ones are mere flights of fancy. Without a sure footing, we run the risk of losing our balance.

Finally, this gift brings the challenge of the gospel life to every crossroads. It reminds us that our baptismal promise to imitate Jesus' life of peace, love and justice must be actively and intentionally pursued as we "vote with our feet." With the gospel as a pilgrim's guidebook, every decision becomes an expression of Christian discernment.

The Spirit's gift of counsel puts into perspective the crossroads before us with its different directions. It gives us hindsight into the past, insight into the present and foresight into the future as we continue our pilgrimage over the horizon.

For Reflection

- *When did counsel help me to truly respond to a situation when I was initially tempted just to react to it?*

- *When did counsel give me hindsight into the past, insight into the present and foresight into the future?*

- *In what areas of my life do the gift of counsel and the gospel challenge me to stretch the limits of my horizon?*

O SPIRIT OF COUNSEL, faced with difficult decisions, I have often chosen the candlelight of hidden motives and wrong reasons. To stand in counsel's floodlight seemed too blinding for my weak vision.

With your grace as a lamp to my feet and a light to my path, illumine the crossroads of my life so that my choices reflect realistic dreams and radiate a future of hope.

May your gift of counsel enable me to abandon to your mercy my past poor decisions, abide confidently in the present and become more available to others as we journey together toward the dawn.

I ask this blessing in the name of Jesus, Light of the World. AMEN.

CHAPTER SEVEN

The Gift of Fortitude

At the beginning of the first millennium, brave men and women witnessed to Christ in a heroic way, knowing full well their words would lead them to the lions' jaws.

In the thirteenth century, Clare of Assisi stood up to the pope and insisted upon the right to live a life of absolute poverty, a privilege she initially had been refused.

During the late 1960's, while he lived as a hermit, Thomas Merton gave retreats to peace activists and wrote ardently against the Vietnam War, much to the chagrin of his Trappist community and some Catholics.

In a stunning gesture that would ultimately lead to his assassination, Israeli Prime Minister Yitzhak Rabin shocked many in his country by deciding to negotiate peace with the Palestinians.

Last year, Amanda became very uncomfortable with the sexually suggestive jokes her friends liked to tell during the lunch period. She surprised even herself when, instead of turning a deaf ear, she confronted and stopped a friend from telling a joke he had heard over the weekend.

Early Christian laity. A woman of nobility. A Trappist

monk. A Jewish politician. A high-school freshman. They are very different people who lived in very different times. And yet, they all shared the courage and conviction that comes from the Holy Spirit's gift of fortitude.

Strength for the Heart

The fifth gift of the Holy Spirit, as the Latin word *fortitudo* suggests, is strength. Its synonym, courage, reminds us that it sinks its roots deep down into the *heart* (*cor*), that interior place where we engage and experience life. Indeed, it is a vitamin shot that nudges us out of the shadows of self-doubt and releases us from the grip of fears that often paralyze us from standing up, speaking out and doing what we know is right. It emboldens us to witness to the truth without compromise.

Fortitude lights a "fire in the belly." It transforms ordinary people into prophets who stand up for what is right and defend their convictions, even when they must swim against the tide. Whether they are cutting through national agendas and looking to the good of the global community or challenging unjust practices even in the Church, these people stand firm and hang tough. They are not afraid of being ridiculed, misunderstood or even blackballed, though they have nothing to gain and everything to lose.

Sometimes, however, taking a stand for the truth is easy and comes naturally. But after we have drawn the line and spoken up, reality sets in, and we become aware of the consequences of our words and actions. What do people think of me now? Did I look like a fool? Have I lost my friends?

Fortitude gives us the determination, assurance and confidence to follow through with our decisions. We give little consideration to the backlash or the clouds of second-guessing that sometimes roll in after the sun sets.

Strength Against the Shadow

Last year, a friend of mine became aware of some personal issues that were getting in the way of living life to the full. They were causing obstacles in the relationships with her spouse, family and friends, and driving her into confusion and depression. She subsequently made the brave decision to go for counseling. She's been in therapy now for more than five months and has often written me, saying it's hard work. She finds herself battling against discouragement. "Struggling with these issues causes me so much pain, I sometimes wonder if it's worth it to continue," she recently wrote.

Thanks to the spiritual courage poured out upon her by the Holy Spirit, my friend continues to find the wherewithal to look at her brokenness and confront the shadow side of her personality. Like a contemporary Saint George, she valiantly fights against the personal dragon that is causing havoc in her soul. She refuses to admit defeat and run away.

My friend's temptation toward discouragement reminds me of my own struggles. How often have I found myself slipping into the old routine of manipulating others, lying to protect my ego and turning a deaf ear and a blind eye to the injustices committed against those who have no voice in society? Tired of fighting against them, I find myself at times deliberately choosing to toss in the towel and become comfortable with my sins.

Fortitude gives me a "second wind" to pick up the towel, wipe off my face and get back in the ring to battle my personal demons. Changing bad habits and overcoming sinful behaviors can be slow, but with the Holy Spirit's gift, I find the encouragement and stamina to begin again. Victory is measured in taking the step forward, not in the size of the stride.

Whether it is the fears that circulate around a prophetic stand or the discouragement that sometimes arises as a result of daily struggles, fortitude gives us a touch of invincibility and courage as we claim our identity as followers of Christ: "See, I have given you authority to tread on snakes and scorpions, and over all the power of the enemy; and nothing will hurt you" (Luke 10:19).

For Reflection

- *What personal dragons do I need to face and slay? How can fortitude help me?*

- *When did fortitude give me the courage to swim against the tide and respond to global injustice?*

- *What role does peer pressure play in my life and relationships? In what ways do I need to stand firm and hang tough?*

O GOD OF FORTITUDE, to "go with the flow" I often say what pleases others to avoid confrontation and to make friends. Shrinking from standing up and speaking out, I wade in fear and compromise. Buoyed by my inflated ego, it is easy to float along life's waters.

Come with your gift of courage and enable me to swim against the tides of peer pressure and public opinion. Empower me to face the currents of global injustice and the world of my personal demons. When my arms weaken and my breath runs out, promise me a second wind so that I may never tire of doing what is right and good. AMEN.

CHAPTER EIGHT

The Gift of Piety

"When did you know you were in love?" I asked. "It certainly wasn't love at first sight with bells and whistles going off," Jim replied. "We met in our third year of college. We were taking the same statistics course. At first, we would go out for a quick lunch. I quickly discovered that I really enjoyed Bridget's company. So we started going out on dates—to have a meal together, then to see a movie or go to a dance.

"I was really taken up with her incredible generosity and charity toward others. I still remember being so impressed with the way, after midterms, she would help a struggling classmate on Saturday mornings with the stats course. And, of course, my parents liked the idea that she was a good, practicing Catholic. I wasn't into the 'religion thing.'

"I remember the night she told me that she had noticed me during our first year of college. That's when Cupid's arrow struck me. It confirmed what I had begun to suspect and what she had never said so forthrightly— that she had been watching me all along. That was the first night I told her that I was in love with her. And I guess the rest is history, as they say.

"It's surprising that I started going to church with

her on Sundays—not because I wanted to impress her, but because I found myself caught up in whatever interested her. And what I heard at Mass led to my involvement in volunteer work. Bridget's love seemed to get the ball rolling in my life."

Jim's account is a good analogy of how the Holy Spirit "gets the ball rolling" in our lives with the gift of piety.

The Womb of Passion

The Spirit's sixth gift—piety—is actually a translator's attempt to come to grips with one word used twice. It is only found in the later Greek Septuagint and Latin Vulgate translations of the Old Testament. The Greek word *eusebia* means "godliness" and "devotion." The Latin word *pietas* gives the added nuance of "responsibility" and "a sense of duty and devotion."

As both words suggest, the gift of piety ignites the fires of the spiritual life. It is the spark that comes out of nowhere and sets a person ablaze with love—love of God and love of neighbor. They are the quintessence and elixir of the spiritual life (see Romans 13:10 and 1 Peter 4:8) and the great challenge and responsibility for those who follow Jesus (see Mark 12:29-31). Piety is the womb of passion.

Piety quenches the "spirit of slavery" that lives by do's and don'ts, fearing the fires of hell, and enkindles within us the "spirit of adoption" that knows and experiences God as "Abba!" (see Romans 8:15). We become aware of the fact that we are unquestionably and unconditionally the beloved children of God. Like Jim, we discover we have been noticed all along.

Abandonment

Because of this graced reality, spending time in prayer becomes a real need that flares up in our daily lives. We don't fan the flames of divine love; we simply bask in their warmth. Hesitations and fears go up in smoke as we take the plunge into the present moment and confidently abandon ourselves into the hands of God, knowing full well that "all things work together for good for those who love God" (Romans 8:28).

This gift not only centers us in the here and now, pregnant with divine love, but it paradoxically drives us out of our self-centered lives into the outstretched arms of the poor, the needy and all God's children. Unlike superficial, pharisaical devotion, which simply scorches the surface with external pietistic practices, the Spirit's piety rages beneath the skin and transforms our hearts into furnaces of justice, mercy, faith and love (see Matthew 23). We love others not because we "have to" or "should" but simply because we live with the awareness of being loved. As John writes so beautifully, "We love because [God] first loved us" (1 John 4:19).

Embers of Eden

Furthermore, this inner fire of love lit by the gift of piety leaps out into all creation. Creation is God's ongoing gift and daily commitment to care for our basic human needs and to nourish us physically, psychologically and emotionally.

Consequently, the pious person has a burning passion to protect the environment. Air and water quality, the respectful use and conservation of our planet's natural resources, such as coal, trees and precious gems and metals, and the threatening extinction of endangered species are issues that glow red hot within the heart of God's beloved. One cannot love God and allow the embers of Eden to smolder and go out.

The Spirit's gift of piety sets the world ablaze with love: "Come, Holy Spirit, fill our hearts! Enkindle within us the fire of your love."

For Reflection

- *What sparks "got the ball rolling" in my life of faith? When I realized that God notices me, how did my life change?*

- *What do's and don'ts enslave me? What areas of my life does piety nudge toward freedom and love?*

- *What "flames" bring passion to my life? How can I become a furnace of mercy and justice in the world?*

O FIRE OF LOVE, enkindled with your gift of piety, I long to remember the fires of my life, to rediscover the tiny sparks that seemed to come from nowhere, yet set my heart ablaze. May they become kindling for the present, stoking within me the history, mystery and majesty of your abiding love.

Burning Spirit, free me from the slavery of my self-imposed do's and don'ts so that you do not blow on the embers of a frightened heart. Fan your love within me and teach me to bask in its warmth.

Transform my life into a furnace of mercy and justice. Let me stretch out my hands and find your flame in my fingertips. Only then will I burn with passion and become fire for your kingdom. AMEN.

CHAPTER NINE

The Gift of the Fear of the Lord

"That's O.K.," I responded, "I'm quite content just to look from over here."

The mere thought of accepting Bill's invitation to follow him into the restricted area of the zoo and actually pet the tiger sent shivers down my spine and gave me sweaty palms. I was afraid the big beast would sense my fear and decide that I would make a nice afternoon snack.

"Rex is really a pussycat, in more ways than one," Bill said, knowing my apprehension about getting near the tiger. "He's a Bengal tiger and, like all tigers, a member of the cat family. Most people don't know it, but tigers tend to be solitary animals, coming together only to mate or to share a kill."

I swallowed deliberately upon hearing the "kill" word.

Bill was Rex's caretaker. I watched him as he slowly approached "this ferocious feline," to use his words. He made a point to announce his presence and not do anything that would startle or arouse the tiger's suspicions. Bill had great respect—it came across to me almost as reverence—for this 500-pound animal.

"I still remember the day," Bill confided, "when Rex took a swipe at me. It was a thunderbolt that woke me up."

It was clear that, despite his consoling words to me, Bill knew exactly where he stood in the presence of this powerful animal: faithful caretaker and yet potential prey.

This experience is a contemporary parable to explain the meaning of "the fear of the Lord."

Misunderstood Gift

Many of us have misconceptions about the seventh and last gift of the Holy Spirit. They are often based upon the mistaken belief that a dangerous and deadly deity is stalking us as prey.

The problem mainly lies with the English word *fear*. We think it literally means we must keep our distance and be afraid of God in the same way that I did with Rex. Suspecting God to be a legalistic lawgiver or nitpicking judge, we just assume "it is a fearful thing to fall into the hands of the living God" (Hebrews 10:31).

But the traditional meaning of "the fear of the Lord" has nothing to do with anxiety, dread or trepidation. Rather, in the words of the more accurate translation used during the Sacraments of Baptism and Confirmation, this gift is really the response of "wonder and awe" to God's presence, action and manifestation in our lives. In a word, *fear* means "fascination."

We discover the world of microbes existing under

the lens of a powerful microscope. We gaze upon the oddity of a Venus flytrap. We marvel at the tiny fingers of a three-month-old fetus. We are caught up in distant, unnamed specks of light seen with the aid of the Hubble telescope. We are moved by the eucharistic presence of Christ or the sacramental expression of God's forgiveness. In all such realities we contemplate, we are stunned to realize they have all been created and given as gifts to us by our loving Creator.

The fear of the Lord spontaneously arises from an experience of the Creator's majesty, splendor, grandeur and generosity. It is our natural response to catching a "lightning glimpse" of God's incomprehensible Otherness. Just as Bill realizes every time he stands unprotected in front of that Bengal tiger, our glimpse of God's Otherness reveals just who we are and where we stand: another infinitesimal speck in this vast universe and yet, individually noticed and loved by the Creator.

Wonder and awe are the fruits of our existential poverty enriched by the lavishness of God.

Beginning of Mysticism

This gift also reminds us that the fuse of mysticism has been lit. Like others before us, we occasionally experience God in prayer as light, fire, water, tears, silence and, of course, love. On these special occasions, God takes the bold initiative, draws close and enters our space in a unique way.

As a result, depending upon our individual temperaments, we might "glow hot," burn within, feel enlightened or refreshed, be stunned into silence or be moved to tears of joy before God's presence. We walk away from such experiences touched—even shaken.

We know the God we have just encountered is, in the words of Francis of Assisi, "unchangeable, invisible, indescribable and ineffable, incomprehensible, unfathomable, blessed and worthy of all praise, glorious, exalted, sublime, most high...." (Rule of 1221, chapter 23).

The gift of wonder and awe literally disengages a person from the ego. I am lifted out of "me" as my entire attention is riveted upon "Thee." While I am caught up in Someone far greater and more powerful than myself, I simultaneously realize an important lesson of spirituality: There is more to life than my little world.

No wonder Scripture says, "The fear of the LORD is the beginning of knowledge" (Proverbs 1:7).

For Reflection

- *What experiences of God in prayer have touched my life? How did I deepen in the gift of the fear of the Lord?*

- *What marvels of creation lead me to reverence and awe?*

- *When was the last time I experienced God's presence, action and manifestation in my life? What emotions arose within me?*

GOD OF WONDER AND AWE, I lift my hands as I gaze on all the wonders you have made. I see you in the sky, feel you in the wind and smell you in the lily. All creation manifests your infinite majesty and splendor.

But my praise is empty without service. Desiring to be your blessed and shared presence on this earth, I stretch out my hands in generous giving to minister to those I love and those I don't. May this be a sign of my commitment to you.

Believing you notice me, I open my hands in trusting surrender to your presence. May my little world become the realm of your boundless love and my life a reflection of your lavish generosity.

In praise, service and surrender, I ask you, O Most High God, to deepen in me your gift of the fear of the Lord. AMEN.

CHAPTER TEN

The Fruits of the Spirit (Part One)

Charles has been angry for years about his denied promotion. He continues to gossip about the boss whenever the opportunity avails him. He will tell you frankly that he is stuck in a grudge—and will tell you just as frankly that he is "quite content" to remain that way.

Rose, in her mid-sixties, is one of those rare individuals who has aged gracefully. Despite the murder of her only daughter and the divorce her husband demanded after thirty-five years of marriage, there is not an ounce of bitterness inside of her. She is more concerned about the second-graders at the local grammar school where she volunteers weekly than she is about eliciting someone's sympathy and pity.

Charles and Rose are next-door neighbors and yet they live worlds apart.

Two Kinds of Living

In the Letter to the Galatians, Paul distinguishes between two contradictory life-styles.

The first, called life "according to the flesh," is rooted in the ego. It expresses itself in an overemotional investment in what we do, what we have and what people think of us. As it does in Charles's life, it lures us into bad habits or addictions, patterns of sin or complacency, old grudges or prejudices. It insists upon controlling, manipulating and dominating. Its concerns are selfish, individualistic and superficial.

Paul specifies some of its characteristic actions: "fornication, impurity, licentiousness, idolatry, sorcery, enmities, strife, jealousy, anger, quarrels, dissensions, factions, envy, drunkenness, carousing, and things like these" (Galatians 5:19-21).

The second life-style, life "according to the Spirit," puts a new center of gravity into one's life: the Holy Spirit. Like Rose's life, it is a life-style chosen for others, not in spite of them. It promotes relationship, respect and reconciliation. It concerns itself with a constructive engagement with the world in such a way that we are restored to the paradise of Eden and share in the grace of Christ (see CCC, #736).

The full flowering or fruition of this life-style, according to Paul, is: "love, joy, peace, patience, kindness, generosity, faithfulness, gentleness, self-control" (Galatians 5:22–23). The fourth-century Vulgate translation of the Bible by Saint Jerome adds "goodness, modesty and chastity." Paul's use of the singular noun "fruit" to describe these suggests that they are all dimensions of the same one reality—guidance by the Spirit (see Galatians 5:25).

Spiritual Brick Walls

The vocation of every Christian is to be free. "For freedom Christ set us free" (Galatians 5:1). If we are guided by the Spirit, we will achieve this goal since, as Paul reminds us elsewhere, "where the Spirit of the Lord is, there is freedom" (2 Corinthians 3:17).

To journey with the Spirit is to move beyond excessive fear and selfish desire, those two brick walls anyone struggling to break out of a life according to the flesh encounters. All the great religions of the world testify to the fact that these two emotions often corner us and enslave us. Until we can break through fear and desire, we are not free. Let's look at fear.

Fear constricts us and can even cripple us. It wraps its tentacles around our hearts, raising doubts and what-ifs, and causes us to hesitate—sometimes even to the point of paralysis. Like caged animals, we become listless—a clear sign that we are not living life to the full. Fear freezes our hopes and dreams.

Fear places us in a defensive posture. Walls go up as we become suspicious of others and suspect them of ulterior motives and intentions. It comes as no surprise that fear lies at the root of prejudice and war.

Fear also casts its long shadow on our faith lives. We are afraid of the Sacrament of Reconciliation, apprehensive that we will experience the priest's wrath rather than God's mercy. We doubt the providence of God and the divine ability to provide us with daily bread. Thus, we sometimes become insensitive and greedy, hoarding our loose change and closing our eyes to the outstretched hand of the beggar.

Freedom From Fear

To be guided by the Spirit is to be lifted over the brick wall of fear and planted in the land of freedom. We begin to live life the way God intends.

The fruit of *peace* places us in an open posture of trust and respect, recognizing our former enemy as our brother or sister. It joins *patience, kindness* and *gentleness* in dissipating any repressed anger we might harbor towards ourselves or others who are different from us. Peace recognizes that, in spite of our different appearances and cultures, we are all very much the same, trying to do the best we can. The tributary of peace flows from the river of *love*.

Love begins with the self. This fruit reminds us that guilt and regret are not swamps through which we must wade forever. Rather, the celebration of God's mercy and forgiveness lifts us out of these muddy waters and places us on firm ground where all God's children have been securely rescued.

The fruit of *generosity* breaks the chains of selfishness and greed that fear wraps around our hearts. It emboldens our faith, making us confident that today's table will be adequate. Life according to the Spirit leads us among the poor, the needy, the homeless and the hungry. We continue our journey with open hands, freely accepting and freely sharing as the situation demands.

Guidance by the Spirit breaks the stranglehold of fear which grips us when we live according to the flesh.

For Reflection

- *What fears grip me and cast shadows on my faith?*

- *In what areas of my life am I still living "according to the flesh"?*

- *When do I find it difficult to live in the Spirit's center of gravity?*

O FREEING GOD, I peer over my heart's wall and, bound by fear's tentacles, glimpse the long shadows they cast on my faith. Yet, preferring to live individualistically and superficially, perhaps I am the one who holds fear tenaciously in my grasp. Letting go means living in vulnerable relationships and unreserved forgiveness.

Grace me with the fruits of your Spirit so that I courageously release my grip. Open my hands and, with your gentle guidance, teach me to dismantle the bricks that wall me in and patiently form them into a path that leads to generosity and inner freedom. AMEN.

CHAPTER ELEVEN

The Fruits of the Spirit
(Part Two)

During the Chinese New Year holidays in January, I returned to the States for a three-week vacation. While home, Steven tracked me down. He wanted to come over for a visit.

The last time I had seen Steven was more than six years ago. I was in the midst of packing for China and he was in the midst of marriage preparations in his local parish. I presumed by now he would be firmly established in his law practice and perhaps even have a child or two.

"How's Teresa these days?" I asked.

"Teresa?" he asked with a blank face. "Oh! Teresa! I really don't know. I haven't seen her in over four years."

"Really?" I asked. "I thought the two of you were going to get married."

"So did I," Steven replied. "But in the course of our marriage preparation, I came to a startling discovery. I wasn't so much in love with *her* as I was with the idea of *being in love*. So I decided to call off the engagement."

I realized again just how easily desire can play tricks on us.

Misguided Desire

There is a hole in the heart. There is a crack in the soul. Many times we're not even aware of it, but it's very much present. We often experience it as restlessness and unfocused emptiness. It lies behind a multitude of our actions and motivations. So much of what we think and do are a direct result of our attempts to patch the crack, to fill in the hole.

Desire is the emotional magnet that attracts a multitude of things to satisfy the restlessness caused by the soul's incompleteness. In its mature form, it leads us to reach far beyond ourselves and to open up to a relationship with God. In the famous words of Augustine of Hippo, "You have made us for yourself, O Lord, and our hearts are restless until they rest in you." Indeed, desire is the flint of relationships, the seedling of faith.

Unfortunately, life according to the flesh (see Galatians 5:19–21) twists and distorts a mature desire. It transforms mature desire into a craving, an inordinate attraction, a misguided longing—sometimes well-defined, sometimes very indefinite.

Consequently, we become obsessive and possessive. The hole in the heart becomes a delusional black hole, sucking into itself people, possessions, power and prestige. Our lives become stuffed with trifles and trinkets—a visible sign that we are not satisfied. If we are not careful, the hole becomes a bad habit or terrible addiction.

Life according to the Spirit with its accompanying fruit (see Galatians 5:22–23) unmasks misguided desire and names it as the dangerous poison that it is. It teaches us how to relate to people and possessions in a positive, respectful way without sinking into the quicksand of obsessions and addictions.

The Blessings of the Fruits

Modesty and *chastity* show us how to glorify God with our bodies (see 1 Corinthians 6:20). They teach us that people have names, histories and commitments that must be respected. Other people are not objects of our selfish desires to be taken advantage of, controlled or abused. People we encounter are companions on the journey, not souvenirs to be bought and later tossed away.

Self-control reminds us when enough is enough. It is aware that the body is "a temple of the Holy Spirit" (1 Corinthians 6:19) and shows us how to care for it. It encourages us to take ample time for rest, relaxation and exercise. It also challenges us to get professional help when we find ourselves mired in physical or psychological addictions.

Love and *faithfulness* are two sides of the same coin. They keep our hearts in check. Love nudges us out of our petty concerns and prompts us to sacrifice superficial attractions and selfish wishes. It encourages us to reach out to those with whom we are in relationship—and faithfulness challenges us to stay there. These two fruits discipline our relationships with God and others, making us loyal, devoted, steadfast and trustworthy. The most mature expression of Christian love is commitment.

With the Spirit in the driver's seat, our lives are filled with *peace* and *joy*. These two fruits dissipate the frustration and anxiety which arise when we seek to satisfy our desire to control and manipulate people and events. They foster the habit of bowing before the mysterious questions of the present and responding to every situation with the words of Mary, "Let it be with me according to your word" (Luke 1:38). To be guided by the Spirit is to know that "nothing will be impossible with God" (Luke 1:37).

The Spirit leads us to the one stream that quenches our existential thirst, to the true home which fulfills all our desires—the kingdom of God.

For Reflection

- *How have the fruits of the Spirit helped me deal with my restlessness and unfocused emptiness?*

- *What tricks do my desires play on me?*

- *What still prevents me from reaching beyond myself and opening up to vulnerable relationships with God and others?*

O FAITHFUL GOD, desire plays tricks on me as I attempt to calm my restlessness and fill the hole in my heart with many possessions and unsatisfying pleasures. It's as futile as building sand castles before the tide and as treacherous as quicksand.

Cast your light into my broken heart and encourage me to reach through its crack into the lives of others. With the promised fruits of your Spirit, transform my selfish desires into self-giving love. Bowing in mystery and responding in hope to the marvels of the journey, may I become a faithful companion to others as we make our way home. AMEN.

Growth in the Spirit

Pete was describing some of the lessons he has learned in his five years of marriage to Beth.

"A marriage is like starting a fire in the fireplace. It has to be built, stoked and replenished. You have to be willing to open your heart to someone and become vulnerable. Once you have the fire lit, you have to work hard to keep it going. Marriage doesn't just happen on the big day at the altar—it begins after you leave the reception and have all the thank-you notes written.

"What keeps the fire of marriage stoked and replenished are things like spending time together, sharing feelings and talking over disagreements. It takes honesty. It takes patience. It also takes lots of forgiveness—both of yourself and your spouse. And most of all, it takes the willingness to wake up every day and continue.

"And what has been most surprising is that over a period of time, as I've gotten to know Beth on a deeper and deeper level, I've caught some of her fire and developed interests in the same things that catch her attention. It's really true: Two become one in marriage. It's no longer 'me' but 'us.'"

Pete's experience is the perfect paradigm for what happens as we grow in the Spirit.

God Takes the Initiative

It's so easy to think of the life of faith as simply an intellectual assent to beliefs, teachings, morals, values and head-knowledge of God. But that mind-set really puts the cart before the horse. The life of faith is the process of opening our hearts and entering into a relationship with God, just as Pete does with Beth.

In the spiritual life, God risks the initiative and opens up to us in boundless love by enkindling the flame of the Holy Spirit within us (see Romans 5:5). This Spirit, as the "artisan of God's works" (*CCC*, #741), challenges us to grow deeper and deeper in a relationship with the God who is our divine parent (see Romans 8:15–16), who shares the essence of divine life with us in the Eucharist and who offers unquestioned forgiveness in the Sacrament of Reconciliation.

The Spirit also facilitates our growth by sharing with us divine gifts. Emphasizing the preeminence of God's gift of the Spirit in the life of faith, Paul says, "If we live by the Spirit, let us also be guided by the Spirit" (Galatians 5:25).

But "it takes two to tango," as the old saying goes. Lasting relationships are two-way streets paved with reciprocity and vulnerability. From this perspective, we must take active steps to foster the awareness of the Spirit in our lives, to fan, stoke and replenish the fire God lit. Grace builds upon nature, not in spite of it.

A Two-Way Highway—No Interstate

Being different people, we all relate and express our love for God in different ways, just as I relate to Pete in a way different from Beth. Our Catholic tradition offers an enormous variety of religious practices and spiritual devotions which helps each one of us find our own particular way of relating to God.

And yet the experience of those who have gone before us marked with the sign of faith testifies to the same basic principle: We grow in the Spirit and nourish the flame through prayer.

The foundation of a relationship with God demands spending quality time in prayer. We talk to God, honestly sharing our feelings and impressions of the day. We also spend time in silence, listening to the voice of God that is incarnated in the people and events we experience. This simple dialogue, done faithfully and attentively, helps to keep the gifts and fruits of the Spirit glowing hot.

Daily periods of this kind of prayer make us attentive to the divine in the midst of the ordinary (*wisdom*). We grow in *understanding* of our own and other's actions as we reflect upon our experiences, especially in preparation for the Sacrament of Reconciliation. We come to *know* what's below the surface of daily life, such as the bonds we share with the larger family of creation.

In dialogue with God and others, we discern how to make the right decision for the right reason (*counsel*) and then find the *fortitude* to carry through with it in action. Sometimes the divine presence so blazes up in prayer, in community or in creation that we are stunned into silence, caught up in the lavish generosity of our God (*the fear of the Lord*).

And finally, as we come to know and experience God through the love letter of Scripture and the divine caresses of the sacraments, the fires of love—the gift of *piety*—are fed.

But none of this happens overnight. Indeed, there is no interstate highway to growth in the Spirit. As Pete reminds us, relationships demand patience, forgiveness of faults and, most of all, the willingness to start again with each sunrise.

And ever so gradually, over a period of a lifetime, the fire God enkindled at Baptism consumes a person. *I* becomes *we*. In the words of Saint Paul, "[I]t is no longer I who live, but it is Christ who lives in me" (Galatians 2:20).

For Reflection

- *How do I stoke the fire of the Spirit in my own life?*

- *Which gift and fruit of the Spirit do I most need to cultivate in my life?*

- *Which gift and fruit of the Spirit are most evident in my life?*

O GIFT-GIVING SPIRIT, I often live with my head in the clouds. Give me WISDOM to come down to my heart and experience the extraordinary unfolding in the ordinary. When I am tempted to dismiss others with rushed indifference, grace me with UNDERSTANDING to listen compassionately and to encourage hope and new beginnings. Sometimes the same childhood tape plays in my head. With your gift of KNOWLEDGE, help me to turn down the volume, listen to events and get in touch with what's really going on below the surface of my life. When I am tempted to react, may your gift of COUNSEL enlighten me how to respond instead. Strengthen me with FORTITUDE so that I am not afraid to speak the words of a prophet when I would prefer to whimper. When cold and uninterested, set my heart ablaze with PIETY. When anxiety and apprehension keep me distant, grant me THE FEAR OF THE LORD to approach you in wonder and awe of your caring presence.

O, Holy Spirit, blow on the embers of my soul and reignite your baptismal love in the fireplace of my being. May I bask in its glow while finding you blazing in all creation. One with you and united to the family of every nation and race, may I become your fire in a cold, indifferent world. Empassion my spirit; enkindle my heart. For only if I burn with love will Pentecost rage again. AMEN.